Chang and the Bamboo Flute

ELIZABETH STARR HILL

Pictures by LESLEY LIU

For my daughter, Andrea Hill, and
my son, Brad Hill, with love —E.S.H.

This edition is published by special arrangement with Farrar, Straus and Giroux, LLC.

Grateful acknowledgment is made to Farrar, Straus and Giroux, LLC for permission to reprint *Chang and the Bamboo Flute* by Elizabeth Starr Hill, illustrated by Lesley Liu. Text copyright © 2002 by Elizabeth Starr Hill; illustrations copyright © 2002 by Lesley Liu.

4 5 6 7 8 9 10 0940 16 15 14 13 12 11 10 09

Printed in China

ISBN 10   0-15-356595-0
ISBN 13   978-0-15-356595-3

Chang and the Bamboo Flute

1

Chang's mother moved the charcoal brazier and the wok onto the open deck of the houseboat. She brought out everything she needed to prepare supper. "We're having stir-fried vegetables with ginger sauce," she said cheerfully. "And we have some rice left, and a few lotus seeds."

"Ah! That sounds good!" Chang's father smiled.

Chang tried to look pleased, too, but he saw that there was just one fresh scallion to put in the wok. The other vegetables were dried ones—yam strips, mushrooms, a couple of pep-

3

pers—and the ginger root was slightly mildewed.

Chang knew his parents were not as cheerful as they pretended to be. It had been raining for days. Now, late in the afternoon, it had stopped. A shifting light broke through the heavy sky, but there was still an uneasiness in the air. Lightning streaked above the mountains. Probably it would rain again tonight, and maybe tomorrow, too.

The wet spring was hard on Chang's family, and on many others who lived here along the Li River in southern China. Rice seedlings had been washed out of the paddies. The farmers would have to plant them again. Other crops were rotting in the soggy earth. Food for livestock had grown scarce. And for a cormorant fisherman like Chang's father, every day's catch was a bitter disappointment.

Chang's father owned nine cormorants. In fair weather he went out each day on a little raft, taking most of the birds with him. They were trained to catch fish and bring them back to him.

For thousands of years in China, cormorant

4

fishermen had fished in this way. Usually the fisherman was able to earn a good living, but lately the days of hard rain had turned the water rough and murky. Even when Chang's father took the cormorants on the raft, their sharp eyes could not find many fish.

"I'm glad we can eat out here tonight," Chang's mother said as she lit the charcoal in the brazier. "I'm tired of being cooped up inside."

Chang nodded. The misty air was fresh and cool. He got his bamboo flute, and while his mother cut up the vegetables, he played sharp notes that seemed to echo the sound of the chopping knife. He played. She chopped. They both began to laugh.

Two cormorants, Shen and Kuo, came over to see what was going on. Shen squawked, asking for food.

"Stay back, this isn't for you," Chang's mother told the birds good-naturedly. "And don't get too close to the knife!"

Chang scooped up the glossy black birds and put one on each of his shoulders. They fidgeted nervously. Unsettled weather always made

5

them restless. In his odd voice, Chang told them to calm down.

Chang had been born mute, so he couldn't speak as other people did. But the cormorants had been raised with him on the houseboat. They seemed to understand the croaking, squawking sounds he made. He understood their bird talk, too. Some people called him Bird Boy, and he didn't mind. It was nice, after all, to be able to talk to birds.

"The charcoal's just about ready," his mother said.

She oiled the wok. This was her most treasured possession—a fine steel wok, given to her as a wedding present. Next she seasoned it with garlic and plenty of ginger, and with a dash of soy sauce. Then she added the vegetables.

To Chang, there was a magic in his mother's wok. No matter how dreary the foods were that she put in, something wonderful always came out.

Soon the smell of the stir-fry curled deliciously through the damp air. Chang's father sniffed hungrily.

From the shore, a girl's voice called, "Chang!"

Chang went around to the other side of the boat and saw his friend Mei Mei on the wharf. He waved.

"If it's not raining tomorrow, will you go to the market with me?" she asked. They both enjoyed walking around the outdoor market. Sometimes they bought a cheap game or something to eat. More often they just had a good time looking.

Chang smiled and nodded.

"I'll come by in the morning, then." Mei Mei skipped away on the path toward the farm where she lived.

Chang watched until she was out of sight. He didn't have many friends. He was lonely sometimes. With all his heart, he hoped tomorrow would be clear.

But in the night he heard thunder, and then a lashing of rain. The houseboat, which usually rode steadily on the river, began to rock and dip. Chang knew it was securely moored to the wharf, but he felt a little bit scared. The river had been rising for days. He had never been in a bad flood, but he had heard how dangerous they could be.

Usually the birds stayed out at night, but suddenly Yudi, the youngest of the cormorants, hopped onto his bedcover. Yudi was alarmed by the storm and needed comfort. Chang had helped to raise the little bird, and they had a special fondness for each other. He smoothed Yudi's feathers and told him to sleep now.

The bird settled down. After a while Chang fell asleep, too.

2

Chang awakened early the next morning. Yudi, who was sleeping on his chest, stirred and croaked.

Chang heard his father calling the other cormorants. He looked outside. The river was rough and brown, and dark clouds hung low over the mountains. But the rain had stopped, at least for a while. His father was about to take the birds out for a day of fishing.

When he had rounded them up, Chang's father tied a long grass straw around each bird's neck. The cormorants were used to this. The straws were not tight enough to harm them.

They just kept the birds from swallowing big fish, and would be untied later.

Chang's mother gave her husband a packed lunch and a thermos of tea. "Please come back if it rains hard. The river is very high," she said anxiously.

"I know. Don't worry."

The fisherman picked up his shoulder pole and let eight of the cormorants hop onto it. Yudi was still too young to go fishing with the others, but he hurried out and tried to get on the pole anyway. Kuo, the lead bird, pushed him off, leaving Yudi squawking in protest.

Chang's father jumped onto the raft with the birds. They took their usual places. Then he untied the raft from the houseboat and poled away.

Other fishermen were out on the river now, each with his own birds. Their narrow rafts were all much the same—five bamboo logs lashed together, their ends slightly upturned, with a lantern in the front.

As they headed toward a bend in the river, the men chanted ancient fishing songs. They sang of good weather and a fine catch—although neither seemed very likely on this dark morning.

"Get dressed, Chang," his mother said. "Your breakfast is ready."

While he ate breakfast, Chang played with Yudi. He tossed a cap onto the deck, then a rag, then a sponge. Each time, he told Yudi to get the object and bring it back. This was a training game. The little bird was learning to give these things to Chang in the same way that he would bring fish to the raft someday.

"Chang! Are you ready?" Mei Mei's voice called from the riverbank.

Chang stuffed the last of the rice in his mouth. He tucked his flute under his arm. Mei Mei liked to hear him play.

Yudi flapped his wings and croaked, not wanting to be left behind again. Chang agreed to take him. He put the bird on his shoulder and waved goodbye to his mother. Then he joined Mei Mei where she was waiting.

Mei Mei's dark eyes shone. She was carrying a faded square of blue cloth.

"Let's go to Zhao the trader's booth," she suggested. "I want to trade my old kerchief for something new and pretty." She held up the kerchief and joked, "Maybe Zhao will let me have a fancy watch for this. Or maybe a gold pin." She laughed. Mei Mei had a fine laugh, like a bell ringing. Chang laughed, too.

They followed the path to the market. The ground was mushy under their sandals. At every step, mud squished between their toes. This amused them, and they spattered through the puddles, not caring how much of a mess they made.

The market was crowded. After so much rain, many people were eager to get out to buy and sell. A vendor was doing a brisk business in pork dumplings and almond cakes. The vegetable woman's stand was short of fresh greens, but she had plenty of yams and dried mushrooms and lily buds. The noodle man sang out his wares: "Wontons and rice sticks, noodle nests and bean threads . . ."

Chang's mother had a special way of frying dried bean threads. She always threw the slender noodles into hot oil in the wok, where they puffed up and turned crisp and crunchy. Chang wished he could buy some for her as a surprise, but neither he nor Mei Mei had any money. They hurried on to Zhao the trader's booth.

Zhao was a big man with a scowling red face. Chang felt nervous as they approached him. He knew the trader drove a hard bargain, and that he could be mean if he didn't get his way.

A woman was offering him a teapot. Zhao shouted at her, "What, an ugly teapot for my lacquer box? You must be mad! I'll give you this wooden box in exchange, but nothing better."

"The clasp on that box is missing," the woman pointed out.

"What difference does that make?" Zhao demanded. "It will hold what you put in it—maybe better than that teapot, which has a crack on the bottom."

"That's not a crack, it's a tea stain!" the woman told him.

"And a dirty pot, at that!" Zhao roared.

They haggled for a few more minutes. The trader got angrier and angrier. In the end, the woman handed over her teapot and took the wooden box, grumbling.

Mei Mei and Chang, with Yudi on his shoulder, stepped closer and looked at what Zhao had to trade. The stand was a hodgepodge of dented pots and pans, paper parasols with torn edges, odds and ends of clothing. Most of this was not worth having, in Chang's opinion. But there were a few pretty things mixed in: a little piece of lace, a plastic fern, a curved comb with sparkles set along the top.

"I like the comb," Mei Mei whispered to him.

Chang nodded. He thought the comb would be perfect to hold back Mei Mei's long hair. But he knew that perfect things were hard to get at Zhao's stand. He hoped Mei Mei wouldn't be disappointed.

3

Mei Mei held out her kerchief to Zhao. "I'll give you this for the comb with the sparkles," she said shyly. She spread the kerchief near the edge of the stand so the trader could see it better.

On Chang's shoulder, Yudi watched with interest. The little bird seemed to think this might be like the training game. He leaned forward and tweaked playfully at the kerchief.

Zhao shouted, "Get that nasty bird away from my stand!"

Chang jumped. He moved back and held Yudi still.

The trader put his hands on his heavy hips.

"Used clothes aren't worth much," he told Mei Mei.

Mei Mei swallowed and answered bravely, "I guess used combs aren't either."

"This comb is fit for an empress," the trader said in a wheedling tone.

"The kerchief was given to me by my grandmother," Mei Mei said. "It has very neat stitches around the hem."

Zhao asked, "Have you anything else to throw into the bargain?"

Mei Mei shook her head.

Zhao put his finger on the side of his nose as though considering the situation. "Well, I'm a generous man," he said finally. "Take the comb."

Mei Mei's face glowed like a sunrise. She picked up the comb and turned away, marveling at her new possession.

But a moment later she cried out, "It's broken!" She held out her hands to show Chang. The comb was in two pieces. It had only been glued together to appear whole. Not only that, but several of the sparkles had fallen out when it came apart.

"I don't want a broken comb!" Mei Mei told

the trader angrily. "Give me back my kerchief!"

"You made a bargain," Zhao said in his harsh voice. "You must keep it."

Mei Mei tried to grab the kerchief, but Zhao tossed it farther back on the stand, where she couldn't reach it.

"Awk!" Yudi squawked.

Chang stepped forward. Quickly he told the little cormorant that *this* was the game. He told him to fetch the kerchief *now*.

Yudi swooped off his shoulder, grabbed the blue cloth in his bill, and pushed it proudly into Chang's hand. Chang passed it along to Mei Mei. She dropped the two pieces of comb on the stand, and she and Chang fled, with Yudi flapping around between them.

Zhao shouted after them angrily. Mei Mei and Chang kept running. When they had left the trader far behind, they slowed down, out of breath.

Mei Mei tied the kerchief around her neck. Chang saw she was upset. He plucked a pink blossom from a bush and gave it to her. She stuck it in her hair. He thought it looked just as nice as the comb would have. Maybe better.

As they walked along, thunder rumbled in the distance, and a streak of lightning ripped through the dark sky above the mountains. Chang knew they probably should go home, but neither of them wanted to. And it wasn't raining yet.

"Let's go on to Bo Won's house," Mei Mei suggested.

They followed the path to where the old storyteller lived. Bo Won was blind. He could not farm or fish. On most days, he sat on the dirt floor in the open doorway of his house and told stories to people who stopped to listen. Sometimes they gave him a little money.

When they reached his house, Bo Won was in his doorway, as usual. "Who's there?" he asked amiably.

"It's me, Mei Mei," she told him. "And Yudi and Chang."

"Sit down, sit down," Bo Won invited them.

They sat on the ground. Mei Mei held Yudi on her lap.

"Would you like to hear a story?" Bo Won asked.

"Yes, please," Mei Mei said eagerly.

The storyteller thought for a minute, then began, "Once there was a tortoise named Tong. He moved into a town where no tortoise had ever lived before. The townspeople had heard that tortoises live for a long time and grow very wise, so they looked at him with great respect."

Bo Won went on to say that actually Tong was quite young, and not wise at all. In fact he was rather foolish. But he was good-natured. When people came to him for advice, he gave it readily. He told people whom to marry, what to sell in their shops, and which candidate to elect as mayor. But because his advice was bad, everything went wrong. The townspeople had one misfortune after another.

Still, they thought it must all be their fault because the tortoise was supposed to be so wise.

Then a little girl went to Tong and said, "My teacher never likes the papers I write. What should I do?"

Tong advised the girl not to write papers for the teacher, but to make almond cakes instead.

The girl's mouth dropped open in surprise. "That's the silliest idea I ever heard!" she cried.

Several townspeople were listening, and they

agreed with the girl. They thought of how badly things had gone for them when they did what the tortoise said.

"Why, he's not wise at all!" someone said.

So people turned against Tong. They chased him out of town, yelling at him and throwing stones.

Tong settled in another town, called Kwung Lo. From then on, when people asked his opinion, he simply looked thoughtful and blinked one eye.

"Tong became famed as the Wise Tortoise of Kwung Lo, and was happy and respected for the rest of life," Bo Won ended with a smile. "And that is why, to this day, no tortoise ever gives advice."

Chang and Mei Mei giggled and clapped their hands.

Mei Mei said, "We have no money, but Chang has his flute. He could play you a tune."

Bo Won nodded. "I like music," he said.

The story had put Chang in a lively mood. He played a new tune made up of some of the sounds he liked best—crickets chirping on a

riverbank, nightingales singing in the lychee trees, Mei Mei's laugh.

Sometimes when he played, Chang felt almost as though he were speaking his thoughts. The flute was his other voice. He felt that way now.

"Thank you," Bo Won said when the tune was done.

Mei Mei and Chang said goodbye to the old man. With Yudi, they started on the path toward the houseboat.

They were about halfway there when the rain began.

4

The rain started as just a light shower, but quickly it grew heavier. Mei Mei slipped and fell in the mud. Balancing Yudi on his shoulders, Chang helped her up. They both had trouble keeping their footing in the hard, slanting downpour.

"This is awful," Mei Mei gasped.

Chang made a sound of agreement. They ran on.

Chang glanced at the river. The water was rough, and rising higher by the minute. In one place, it suddenly crept over the bank. Fear clutched at his stomach. If the path went underwater, he and Mei Mei could get trapped, cut off from their homes and families.

Mei Mei saw the danger and cried, "Hurry, Chang! Faster!"

Slipping and sliding, they stumbled forward as fast as they could. But the river kept rising, flowing across the path just in front of them.

Mei Mei and Chang held hands to keep from falling. Chang couldn't see his houseboat yet. He pictured it being torn from its mooring and whirling away. At last they rounded a little turn in the path, and he saw it rocking on the river, but still moored to the wharf.

Mei Mei ran off to the farm where her family lived. Chang jumped onto the houseboat. Yudi squawked loudly, hopped down from Chang's shoulders, and streaked into the cabin.

Chang's mother stuck out her head from inside. "Oh, Chang, I'm so glad you're back!" She came onto the deck. "Now if your father could just come home . . ."

Chang felt a chill. So his father was still out on the little fishing raft.

Chang and his mother stood on deck together. It was hard to see clearly through the rain, but

26

at last Chang could make out the raft in the distance. He saw his father struggling against the rushing river, trying to reach the houseboat.

Slowly the raft was coming closer, but not in a straight line. It was held in the middle of the river by the current. Chang's father kept trying to turn sidewise and head directly to the houseboat, but he couldn't match the force of the current.

The cormorants were huddled around him on the raft. Chang could hear the birds croaking in bewilderment. They weren't used to being out in storms, and they sensed that things had gone badly wrong. Only Kuo, the leader of the fishing birds, seemed undisturbed. As always, Kuo was perched on the upturned prow of the raft, brave and strong.

Chang knew there was a coiled rope on the deck of the houseboat, kept to tie up the raft. He knew, too, that it wasn't long enough to reach to the fishing raft. He felt miserably helpless.

"If only we could get the end of the rope to your father," his mother cried in frustration.

Looking at Kuo, Chang had an idea. It might not work, but he had to try.

From inside the cabin he got his mother's laundry line and tied it to the rope, then fixed one end of the heavier rope to the ring on the side of the houseboat. In his loudest squawking voice, he called Kuo.

The bird looked at him. Of all the cormorants, Kuo was the strongest. But as with the other fishing birds, some of his wing feathers had been clipped to keep him from flying far away. Kuo could take short flights, but the storm would make it harder.

Chang hesitated, fearful again. What if the finest of his father's birds went down into the tumbling river? Would the cormorant be able to get out again, or would he be injured and swept away?

Maybe it was wrong to risk Kuo's life. Yet what choice was there?

Again Chang called the bird.

Kuo flapped his wings and flew from the raft. Chang urged him on. He told the bird that he could do it, he *could*.

Fighting the wind, Kuo gusted up and down like a tattered black kite, crossing the distance between the raft and the houseboat. He landed in a tumbled heap beside Chang on the deck.

Chang wished he could keep the bird with him, but the job wasn't done yet. He praised Kuo. Then he gave him the loose end of the laundry line and told him that he must take it to the fisherman, just as he often took fish.

Kuo seized the line in his beak and returned to the raft. Chang's father grabbed it and tied it to the raft. Chang pulled hard on the other end. His mother helped, while his father started poling again.

To Chang, the raft felt like a giant fish on the end of the line, maybe like the biggest fish in the world. But gradually the three of them turned the raft out of the current. Tugging, pulling, poling, they brought it across the rough water to the houseboat.

Chang wanted to sing, to shout. They had done it!

Chang's father tied the raft to the houseboat. Kuo was the first to hop on deck, followed by the others. Then Chang and his parents and the birds all took shelter together inside the cabin.

To Chang, the sounds of the steadily falling rain and the rocking of the boat were suddenly festive, a delightful departure from the normal calm. He was happy. Why not? They were all safe together!

His mother, who often shared his moods, suggested, "Play us a party tune, Chang!"

Chang picked up his flute. He thought of a funny story Bo Won had told him once, about a ghost who fell in love with a pumpkin and danced with her all night long. Chang could see the dance in his mind.

As he played, the music seemed to leap and twirl, bouncy as the pumpkin, graceful as the ghost. Chang's parents took hands and tried to dance a little, but the cabin was too crowded with birds. Laughing and breathless, they stopped.

Chang finished his tune with a flourish.

His mother said, "I'm hungry. I guess we all are."

Chang nodded vigorously. He hadn't eaten anything since his morning rice, and that seemed a long time ago.

His father said, "We caught some fish before

the storm got bad. Not many, but enough for us all to have a good meal."

He untied the straws from the cormorants' necks and gave them a few of the smaller fish. His mother cleaned the rest. She placed the charcoal brazier outside on the deck, under an overhang of the cabin roof, where it was mostly protected from the rain. Now the cabin would not get too smoky while the food was cooking.

She boiled rice over the charcoal in an old iron pot. Then she put the pot aside and prepared the fish with dried chestnuts and soy sauce and the last of the ginger root. She took out her wok and heated up the cooking oil.

As always, the sight of the wok made Chang's mouth water. His mother added the fish to the hot oil. In a minute it sizzled and smelled wonderful, and in another minute it was done.

The family filled their bowls high, and his mother made tea. As they ate and drank, it seemed to Chang that nothing could be better than this.

5

The birds settled down quietly. Everything seemed peaceful. But under the houseboat, the river rushed and tugged as though it wanted to carry them away. And the rain fell all afternoon.

Chang and his mother kept glancing outside. Normally the wharf was a foot or more higher than the water, but now it was just about level with the river's surface. Chang looked out the other way and saw a child's doll whirling along, followed by a quilt. Later a huge tree branch floated past. Three chickens were sitting on it, clucking nervously. They drifted on, out of sight.

Next a little piglet passed, balanced on a log.

Then a table went by.

Chang stared at all these things in horrified surprise. Where had they come from? Where would they end up? He felt as though he had landed in the middle of a bad dream. He made a croaking noise of dismay.

His mother came and sat beside him. Together they watched part of a broken wharf swinging along on the current.

"The river must have flooded the land, farther upstream." Her voice trembled. "I hope the people are all right."

The next moment, a wooden cart hurtled toward the houseboat, carried downstream like the other things. It was a large produce cart, the kind farmers used to transport their wares to the market. Chang often saw these carts jouncing along on land, pulled by buffaloes. But to see it now, like this, was terrifying. The rushing water upended it, and one of its big wheels was sticking out, heading directly for the cabin.

It was close—closer—

With a dreadful crash, the wheel hit the side of the boat. Part of the cabin was torn away. Giant splashes of water gushed in.

Chang's mother screamed.

His father shouted, "Chang, get all the birds together! We have to go ashore right now!"

As water flooded into the houseboat, Chang rounded up the birds and snatched his flute. The cormorants squawked in alarm. Chang told them not to be afraid, but he was very scared himself.

Chang's father picked up his pole, and the birds jumped on—all except Yudi. Chang tucked the young bird under one arm, his flute under the other, and followed his parents.

The wharf was covered with an inch or two of water now, but they were able to get across to the riverbank. They stood there forlornly. Rain streamed down their faces.

The houseboat bobbed crookedly on the river. Chang saw water sloshing through the cabin and across the deck. A pain grew in his heart. This was the only home he had ever known.

Dusk darkened the sky. The birds croaked anxiously.

"We must find a place to stay the night," Chang's mother said finally. "Maybe Mei Mei's family would take us in."

Chang was upset by this idea. His parents seldom visited with land people. Mei Mei had often come to the houseboat for a meal or to play checkers with Chang, but he had been to her farm only a few times. Her brother, Jinan, always made fun of him, and Chang kept away from him as much as he could. Now, drenched and dirty, he hated the thought of going to the family for help.

He shook his head vigorously.

"Their farm isn't far from here," his mother argued, "and we have to go someplace."

His father was doubtful. "We are asking them to take in three people and nine birds," he said dryly. "Isn't that a lot, on such slight acquaintance?"

Chang nodded, tugging insistently at his father's wet sleeve. But his mother repeated, "We have to go someplace."

"All right," his father said.

With Chang lagging behind, they trudged along the muddy path and up a hill to Mei Mei's farmhouse.

6

Mei Mei answered the door, with her parents behind her.

To Chang's distress, Jinan came from another room. Looking at the bedraggled family, he smiled scornfully. "What happened to you, Bird Boy?" he asked sarcastically. "Did you get dunked in the river?"

Chang turned away. Jinan knew he couldn't answer. That was part of his meanness, to ask questions of a mute boy.

Chang's father explained the situation. "We do not ask to stay in your home," he said politely, balancing the pole full of birds. "But perhaps you have a garden shed . . ."

"We have a large barn," Mei Mei's mother offered. "It is very humble," she added with her own politeness, "but I think you will be quite comfortable there, if you don't mind sharing with our buffaloes."

"Not at all," Chang's mother replied. "We would be most pleased." The two women nodded at each other graciously.

"We'll lend you dry clothes," Mei Mei's father said. "You're soaked."

Chang's parents accepted gladly. The family changed in a back room. Chang was given trousers and a shirt that belonged to Jinan.

Chang felt a prickling shame. Now he was wearing Jinan's clothes, sheltered in Jinan's home. At this minute, nothing of his own was as good as what Jinan had.

"You can keep those if you want," Jinan said carelessly. "I was going to throw them away anyhow."

Chang flushed and gritted his teeth.

"You're all most kind," Chang's mother said.

"See you tomorrow, Bird Boy," Jinan said.

Mei Mei put on a rain slicker and hat and took Chang and his family to the barn. It was warm and dry and cozy, and smelled of hay. Two buffaloes whiffled and steamed the air as the family came in, but then ignored them.

Mei Mei made several trips from the barn to the house, bringing quilts and bowls of food and a large pot of hot tea. Because the farm was on high ground, the buildings had not been damaged, and the past rains had drained off the land without ruining their crops. Her family still had some vegetables in their fields.

"We have no fish for the birds, though," Mei Mei apologized.

"They ate a lot, earlier today," Chang's mother said quickly. "They will be all right."

"Good night, then," Mei Mei said. "Good night, Chang."

After she left them, they ate silently.

At last Chang's mother said, "If the boat breaks up and sinks, where will we go? What will we do?"

"Don't think of that now," Chang's father answered wearily. He finished his tea, pulled off his boots, and stretched out on a big heap of hay. "We can't do anything tonight. Rest."

Chang and his mother nodded. They sat up for a while, listening to the rain. Some of the cormorants settled around them. Others roosted on a low beam, fidgeting restlessly.

Chang still had his flute. He thought it might calm the birds if he played for them. He tapped the flute and looked questioningly at his mother.

She shook her head. "No, your father wants to sleep. And who knows?" She smiled. "The buffaloes might not like it."

Soon they began to yawn. They stretched on the hay beside Chang's father. As Chang drifted off, he heard the voices of the birds, confused and complaining. And *hungry*.

Chang had never spent a night on land before. He missed the constant motion of the boat. He kept waking up when the buffaloes whiffled. Worst of all, he wondered if the houseboat was still afloat, or if it had been torn from its mooring and battered to pieces by the river.

In the morning, Chang's parents went down to the wharf to see what had happened to the boat.

Chang wanted to go, too, but his parents said he had to stay with the birds, who would certainly be upset if the whole family left.

While they were gone, Jinan came to the barn. He asked Chang, "Want to play cards?"

Chang shook his head.

"Guess you're afraid I'll beat you," Jinan said.

Chang turned to the roosting birds. In his squawking voice, he called them. They all swooped down, landing on his shoulders and outstretched arms, flapping around both boys.

Startled, Jinan yelled, "Get them away from me!"

Chang laughed. Jinan ran from the barn.

Soon Chang's parents returned and reported that the houseboat seemed just as they had left it. "We didn't go on board," his father said. "It's not raining so hard now, but the river is still dangerous. We'll have to wait to see how much damage was done."

He borrowed a net from Mei Mei's father and caught a few small fish from the riverbank for the birds. They were used to the bigger fish they could catch by diving into the river, but Chang tried to tell them this was the best that could be done for now. Nets just weren't as good as birds.

The next day the rain stopped, but the flood-waters were still high. Mei Mei and her family urged Chang and his parents to walk up to their house for a visit. "Won't you come and play your flute for us?" Mei Mei's father urged Chang.

Chang shook his head. His music was private and important to him, something to share only with his family and close friends. He felt sure Ji-nan would make fun of it.

Again he remained with the birds. He played games with Yudi and Shen, tossing his sandals for them to fetch.

For the next two days, Chang and his parents stayed in the barn. Mei Mei and her family continued to supply them with meals. They were grateful, but they longed to be home.

Chang was sick of the smell of hay. He could hardly wait to sit out on deck in the marshy air, while his mother cooked supper. He wanted to see the stars again, and to play night music without bothering buffaloes. He was homesick.

At last the river lowered and calmed. The sun sliced through the clouds and glittered on the water.

Chang's father said, "It's safe to go back now."

Both of Chang's parents thanked Mei Mei and her family for their kindness. Then they all squished through the muddy earth back to the wharf.

Smiles spread across their faces as they looked at the houseboat. The damage to the cabin hardly showed from this side. You could almost pretend nothing had happened.

His father said, "I'll go on board first and make sure it's safe." After a moment he called, "It's very damp in here, but steady enough."

Chang and his mother followed. Chang saw at once that the cabin was wrecked. There was a gaping hole in one side. Some of their shelves were gone. Water had soaked their bedding and clothes.

His mother sagged against a wall. Her face was pale and strained. "How can we ever fix this?" Her voice shook.

His father answered slowly, "I don't know."

7

Chang and his parents worked all day. They pried off a loose board and nailed it across the bottom of the hole in the cabin, so the water could not come in. They rinsed wet clothes and bedding and stretched them to dry in the hot sun. They mopped the floor and dried out the cabinet where their small stock of food was stored. They coiled up ropes and folded nets.

As the day went on, Chang's father spoke more hopefully. Soon he would be catching and selling fish again. Little by little, they would earn enough to buy lumber and other supplies to repair the cabin. It might take a long time, but eventually they would make the houseboat as snug and tight as ever.

Chang felt better when he heard this. Maybe things weren't so bad after all.

In the late afternoon, Mei Mei came over, carrying dry charcoal and matches, and a basket of fresh vegetables. "For your first supper at home."

Chang's mother took the basket. Her tired face brightened. "We'll have a grand meal! Thank you, Mei Mei. Please stay and eat with us."

The girl agreed. She and Chang sat out on the deck, swinging their legs. The sun was sinking behind the highest peak of the mountains. Chang's father had let the cormorants free in the river to fish for themselves. The birds splashed in the calm water, sending out showers of golden light.

"Let's go to the market tomorrow," Mei Mei suggested. "It'll probably be a nice day."

Chang nodded, almost contented now. In the river Shen and Yudi played one of their games, tossing a stick. Mei Mei laughed, her laugh ringing like a bell.

Chang's mother cut up the vegetables and started charcoal burning in the brazier. Then she went inside, but in a minute she burst out of the cabin, eyes brimming with tears. "My wok!" she cried. "My wok is gone!"

"Ah, no!" her husband exclaimed. "We must find it!"

He and Chang and Mei Mei crowded into the cabin. The wok had been kept on a low shelf in an alcove. Somehow they still expected to see it there, but now the alcove was empty.

They looked everywhere. It was truly gone.

Stunned, the family realized that when the water swirled in and took out the shelves, it must have carried the utensil away.

Mei Mei thought they should search the cabin one more time. They did, but it was no use. "I'm so sorry," she said miserably. "You know what they say—in a flood, a wicked river spirit always steals something."

But why, Chang wondered, did it have to be the wok? Gladly he would have given up his checkers game instead, or even his kite with the dragon painted on it. He knew how much the wok meant to his mother.

She covered her face with her hands. "We'll never have the money to buy another." She began to cry.

Chang's father put his arms around her. "Boil up the vegetables in your iron pot," he suggested gently. "Supper will still be good."

She got out the old pot and made soup with the vegetables. But none of them felt like eating now. They ate a little, then stopped. Mei Mei went home.

In the night, Chang's mother cried and cried. As he listened, a sharp sorrow stabbed Chang. If only he had money . . . if only he were rich . . .

Usually Chang did not think much about being poor. But now it struck him that so many things were out of his reach.

Once Bo Won had told a story about a poor boy who found treasure in a milk jug, but Chang had never known this to happen in real life.

The next morning Mei Mei came over early. Chang tucked his flute under his arm. He and Mei Mei walked the path to the market. Many other people were out today, smiling and enjoying the sunshine for the first time in days. The end of the flood had brought a holiday feeling to the village.

A tangle of thoughts stirred in Chang's mind. There was one way he might be able to do something for his mother. There was one hard, painful way.

When they reached the market, Mei Mei led him to a row of small shops lining one side of the street. Everything was more expensive here than in the stalls that filled the market square. Mei Mei couldn't afford to buy in these places, but she liked to look in the windows and pretend.

"Maybe I'll get some of those silk flowers," she said with a giggle. "They're much prettier than cheap paper ones."

The next shop had fancy bowls and cups in the window. "Or the rice bowl shaped like a turtle," Mei Mei said.

The last window was full of cooking utensils, including woks. One of these caught Chang's attention. It was even handsomer than his mother's had been. It was bigger, and the handle was made of polished wood. And a lid came with it. His mother's had not had a lid.

Chang wanted this wok desperately, but the price on it made him feel poorer than ever. He moved on. At one of the stalls, Mei Mei bought a small almond cake for each of them.

They were near Zhao the trader's booth. Chang looked over the merchandise. The thoughts that had been stirring in his head grew clearer. He knew Zhao usually had some old pots and pans. Sure enough, amid all the rest of the junk, there was a cheap wok—not fine, not well made, not large. But a wok, at least.

He nudged Mei Mei nearer Zhao's booth.

"I don't want to see that awful man again," Mei Mei whispered. "We don't even have anything to trade."

Chang ignored this. He stepped over to the booth. Hard as it was, he *did* have something to trade. He touched Zhao's sleeve and pointed to the wok. Then he held up his flute.

8

The trader looked at Chang's offering and sneered. "Who would want that? It's nothing but a little bamboo stick!"

"It's not!" Mei Mei said hotly. "It's a flute! And all he wants for it is that old wok!"

"Never!" Zhao said indignantly. "I might give you a box of pencils for it, but nothing more."

Chang shook his head.

"It has to be the wok," Mei Mei repeated stubbornly.

"Well, it won't be!" Zhao retorted.

The argument went back and forth between them, louder and louder. People gathered.

Then a kindly voice asked, "Is that you, Mei Mei?"

Chang and Mei Mei turned to see Bo Won in the crowd. The blind old storyteller hobbled slowly toward them.

Mei Mei answered, "Yes, it's me." Quickly she explained about the loss of the wok and the trade Chang wanted to make.

"I've made you a fair offer," Zhao said. "Pencils for a stick." He laughed heartily.

Some in the crowd laughed, too, but others looked at the flute curiously.

"I'd like to hear a tune," a man called out.

Chang hesitated, embarrassed. Never in his life had he played for strangers. To them his music might be a poor thing, laughable, like his voice.

"Go on, boy. Play," Bo Won suggested quietly.

There was a silence. Chang stood frozen. The group around him was quite large now.

"Play," Bo Won said again, more urgently.

Chang realized that this might be his last chance ever to make music.

Suddenly he didn't mind the crowd. Let them think whatever they liked.

He began to play. At first the notes were shaky, but then they steadied. The melody grew firmer, full of the sounds of his world. They were sounds that belonged to all these people, too. The murmur of the river that gave them a good life, and the drumming of long rains that could take it away again. Breezes in a bamboo grove. The springtime peeping of frogs.

The crowd listened attentively.

Chang went on. He played the ancient chants the fishermen sang as they poled their rafts in the evening.

Some people nodded, recognizing the tunes. They were pleased.

Bo Won untied a kerchief and took out a coin. He threw it at Chang's feet.

Chang was surprised by this. For a moment he didn't know what to make of it. Then he realized it was how people paid the old man to tell his stories.

A few people in the crowd noticed. Now that Bo Won had given them the idea, they, too, stepped forward to throw coins.

"The boy plays well," someone said, and more coins were thrown.

When Chang finally stopped playing, there was a pile of money around his feet.

Zhao cleared his throat. "Well, maybe somebody would like to have the flute, after all," he said grudgingly. "Who can offer me a good trade for it?"

Several people spoke up. But Bo Won advised, "Count your money first, Chang."

Chang scooped up the coins and counted them. He was amazed at how much there was. He remembered the wok in the shop, and saw that he had enough money to buy it.

He had found his treasure, not in a milk jug but inside himself, here in the market square.

He looked at Mei Mei, his face beaming with happiness, and tugged at her arm. They ran to the store. Chang pointed out the wok to the shopkeeper and poured his money on the table.

The shopkeeper counted it carefully, then gave Chang a few coins back. He put the wok in a box. "Would you like to have it wrapped as a gift?" he asked.

Wrapped as a gift! So this was how it felt to be rich! Chang nodded in delight.

The shopkeeper got a fine sheet of paper printed with butterflies.

It pays to shop in a good place, Chang thought.

Outside, the noodle man was calling, "Wontons and rice sticks, noodle nests and bean threads . . ."

Chang still had a little money left to spend, and his mother would need something to cook in her new wok. Fried bean threads! Chang could almost taste them already.